BACK IN THE DAYS COLORING BOOK

Jamel Shabazz

pH powerHouse Books Brooklyn, NY

STARS
PRICE!
38 99
29 99
39 99
39 99
39 99

PRICE!
29 99
PRICE
44 99
PRICE
44 99
NIKE
34

Morgan
spiced Rum!
Love Me

GEORGE'S
JVC

CEE

KANGOL
adidas

phone
PEOPLE

URNITURE
RISING
20
20

THINK
SMACK KILLS

TWICE
ONCE
by:
CHICO
87
163
163
RJ 15